HAL•LEONARD

GUITAR PLAY-ALONG

AUDIO ACCESS INCLUDED

THE VENTURES

CONTENTS

To access audio visit:
www.halleonard.com/mylibrary

4686-0563-1171-5214

ISBN 978-1-4234-7376-3

HAL•LEONARD®

7777 W. BLUEMOUND RD. P.O. BOX 13819 MILWAUKEE, WI 53213

Visit Hal Leonard Online at
www.halleonard.com

Diamond Head

By Danny Hamilton

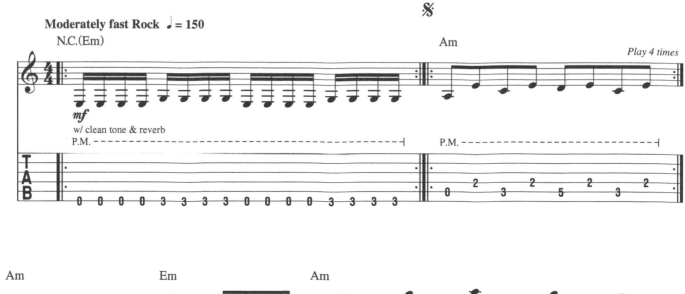

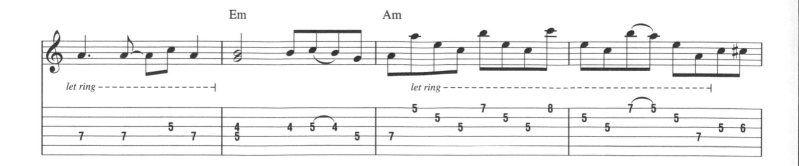

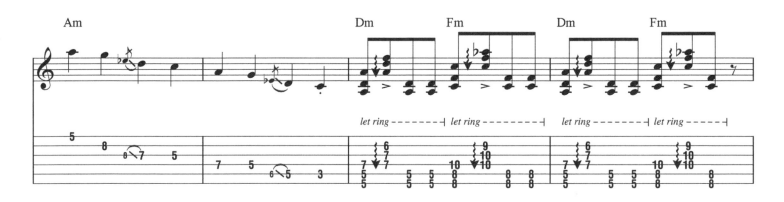

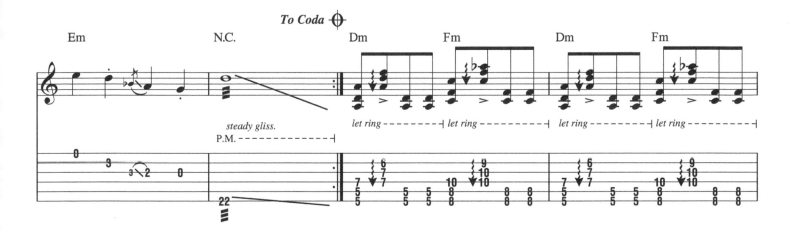

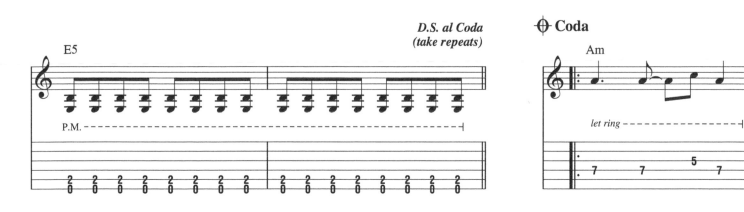

Hawaii Five-O Theme

By Mort Stevens

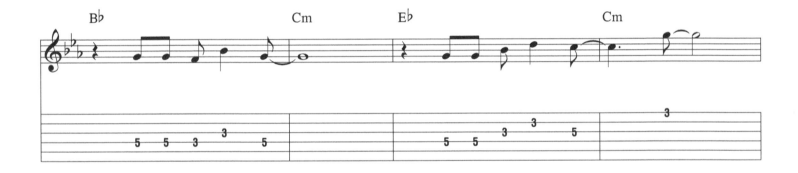

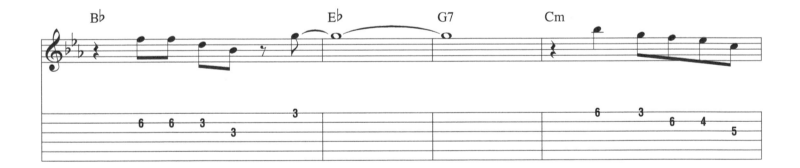

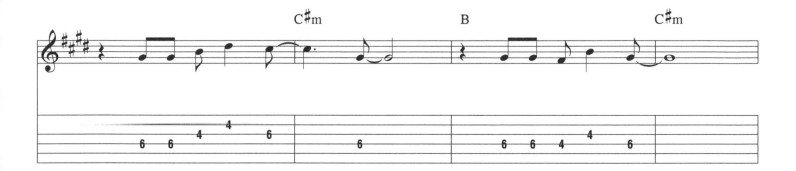

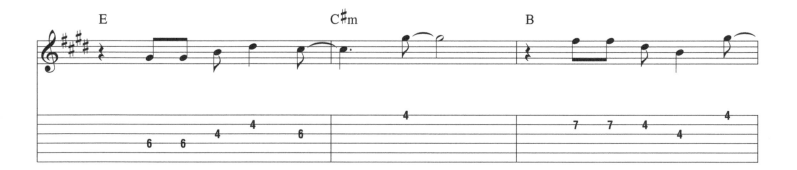

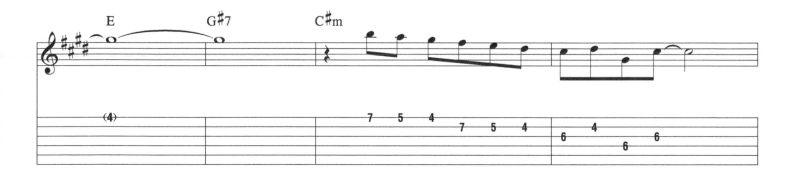

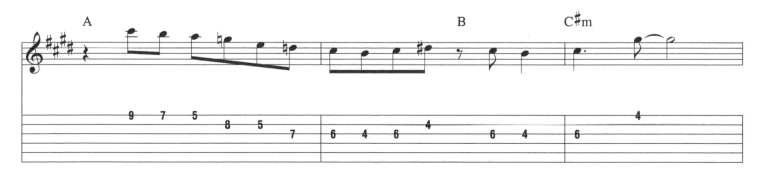

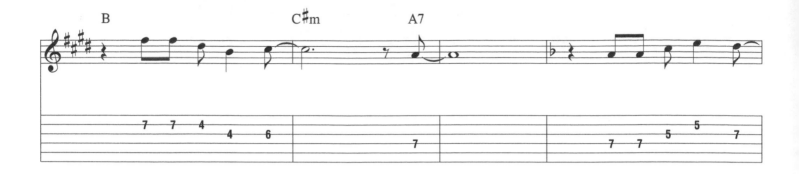

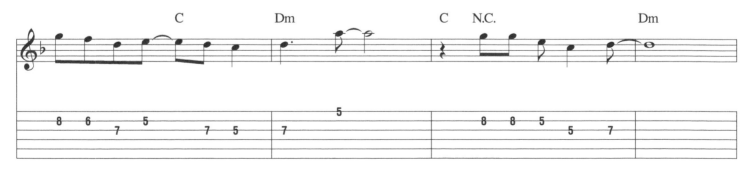

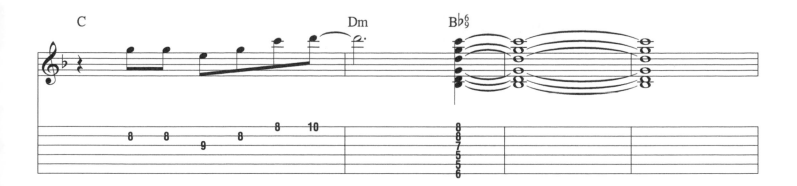

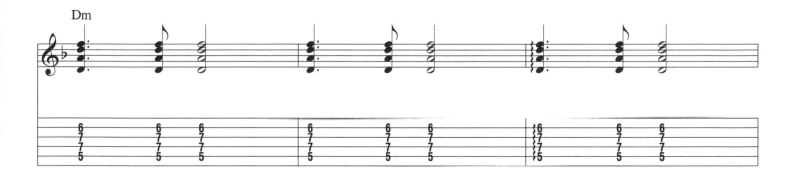

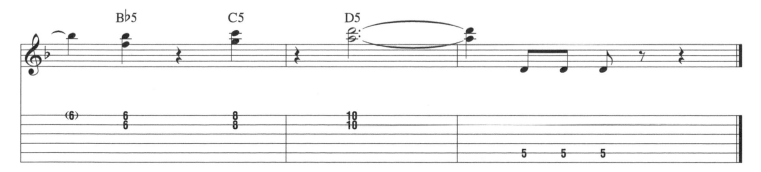

James Bond Theme

By Monty Norman

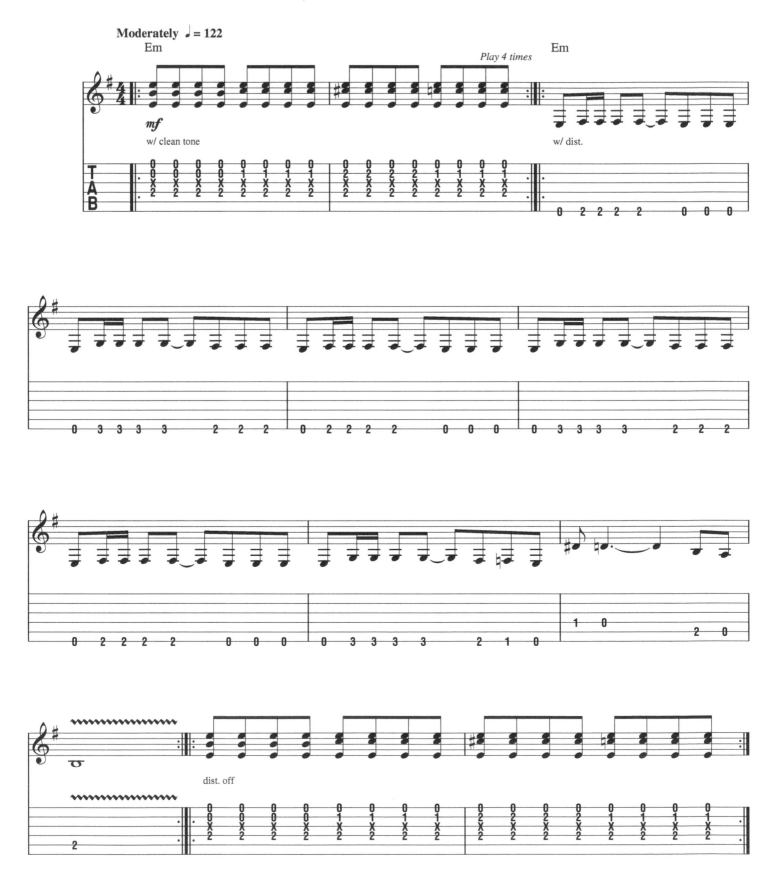

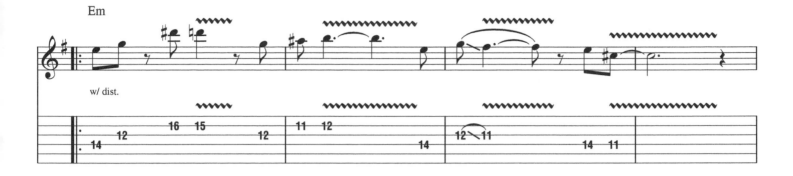

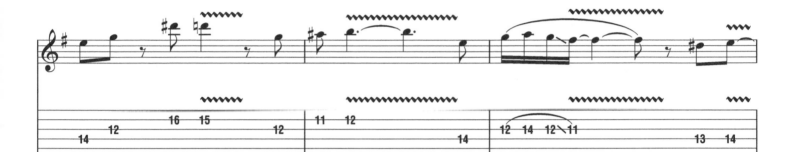

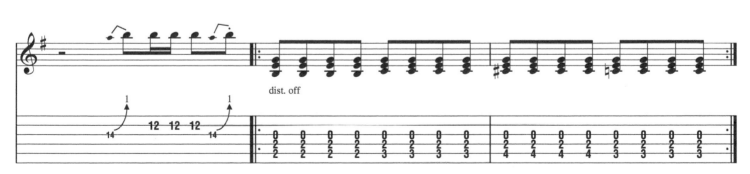

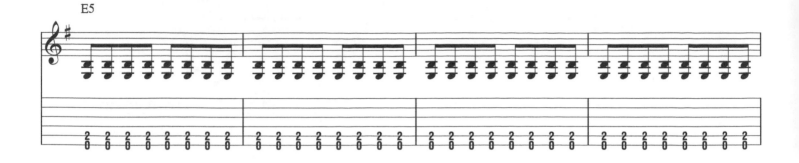

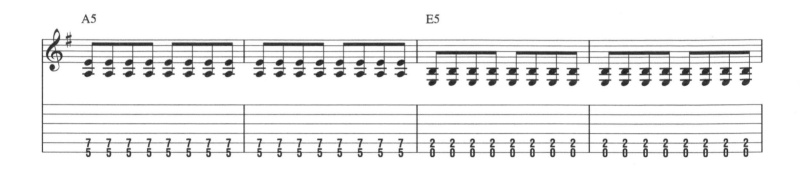

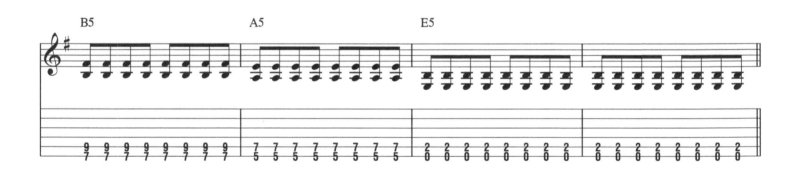

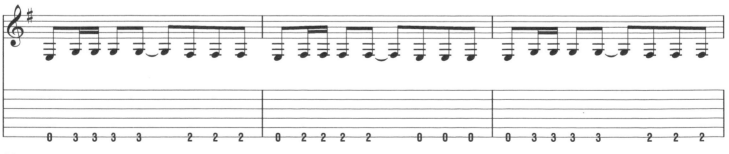

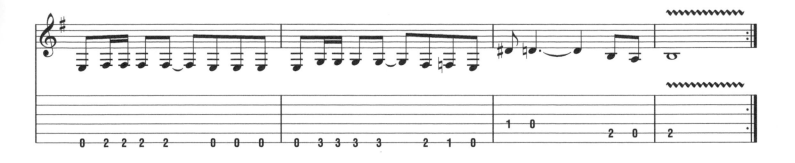

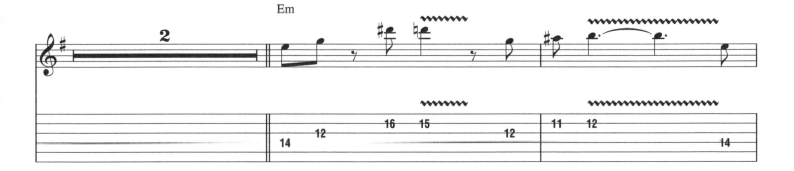

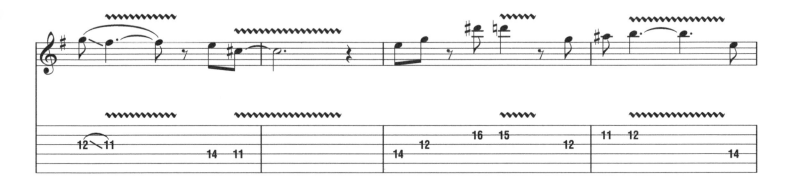

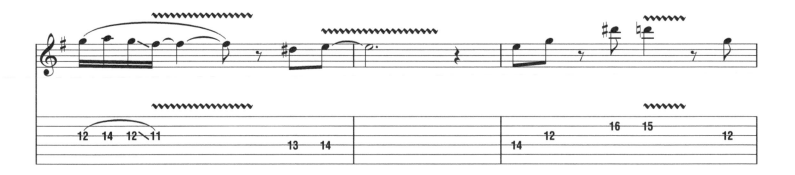

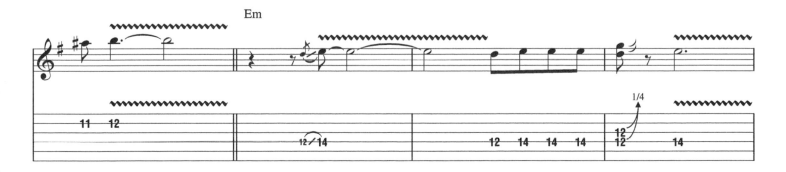

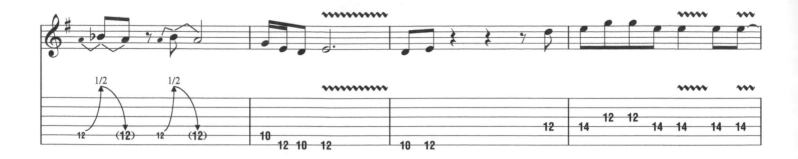

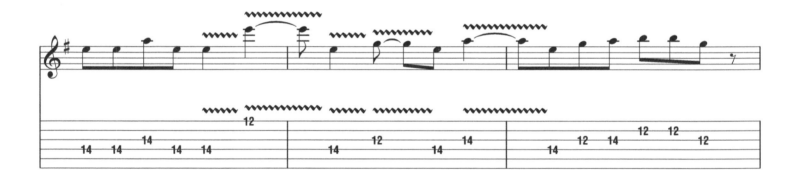

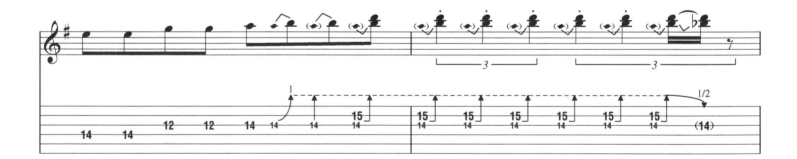

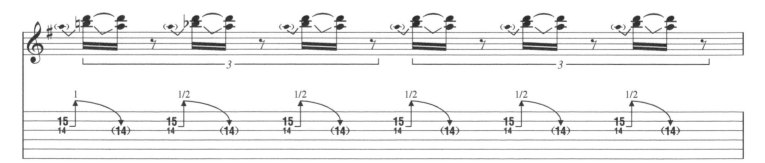

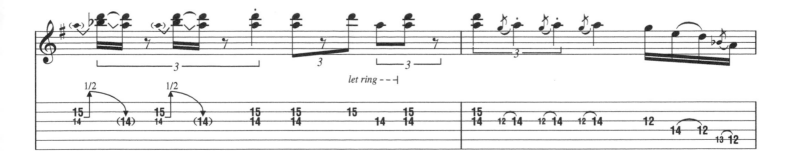

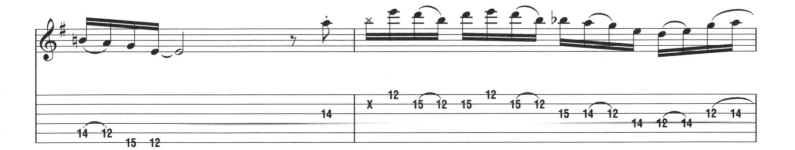

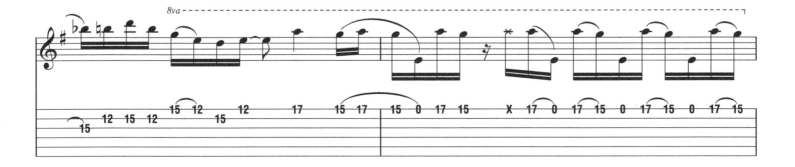

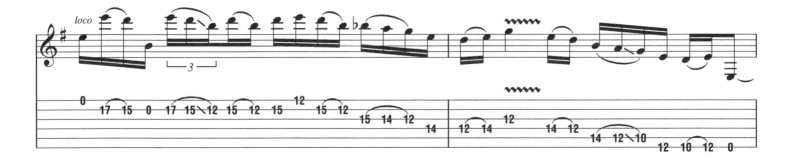

Repeat and fade

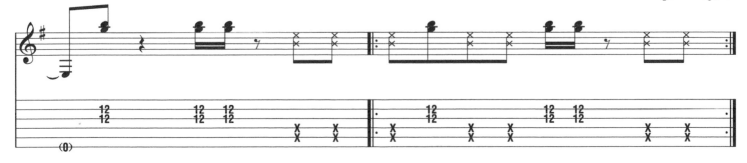

Perfidia

Words and Music by Alberto Dominguez

Intro
Moderately fast Rock ♩ = 154

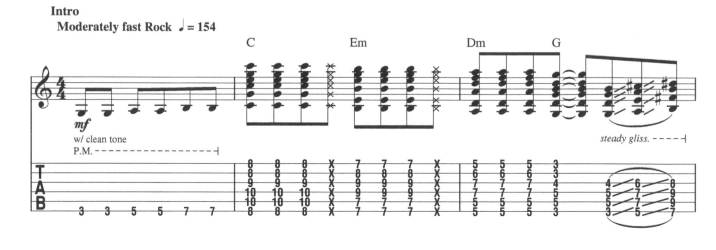

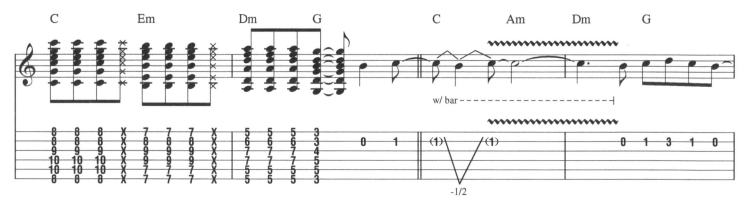

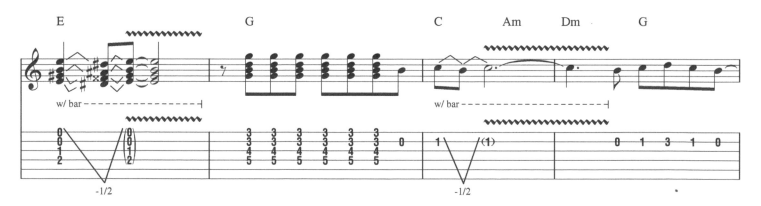

14

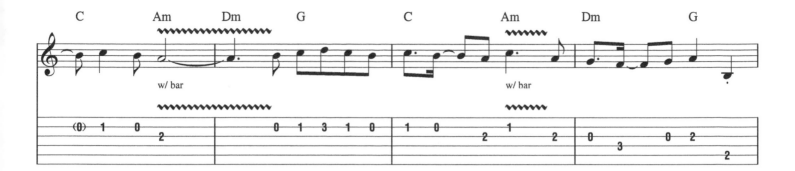

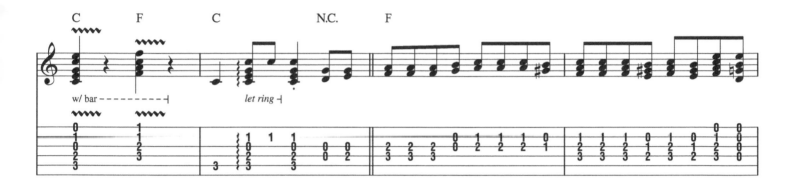

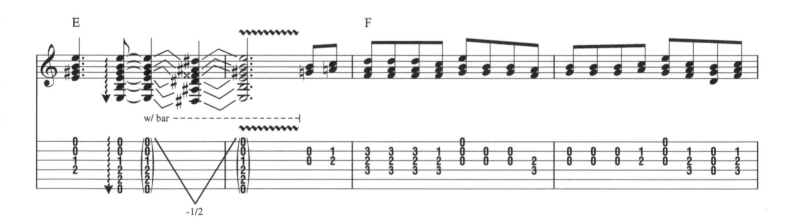

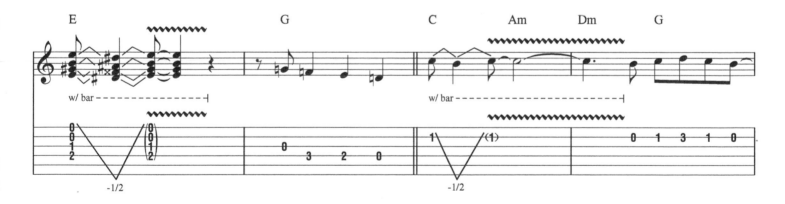

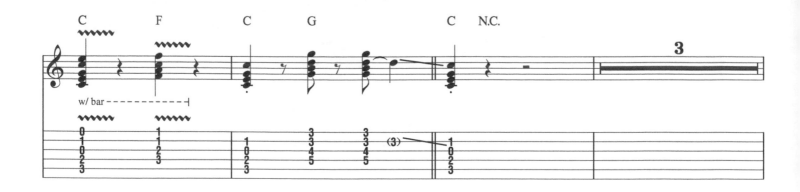

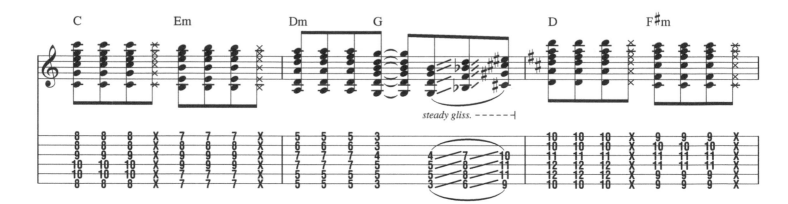

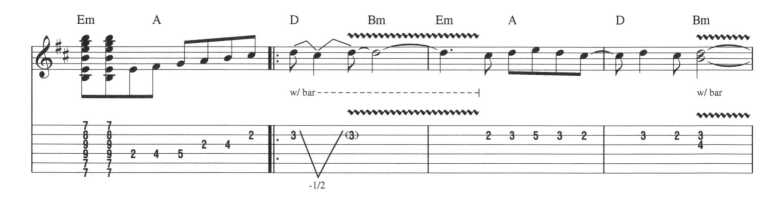

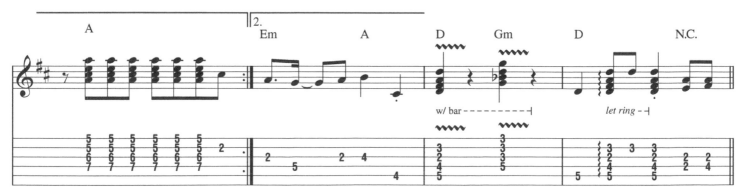

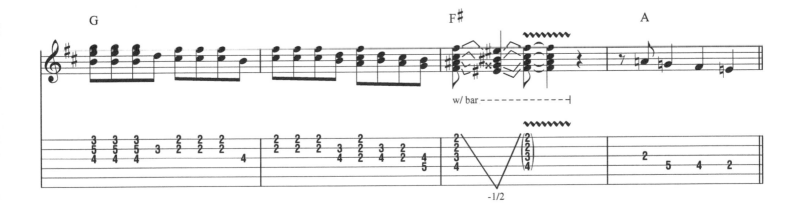

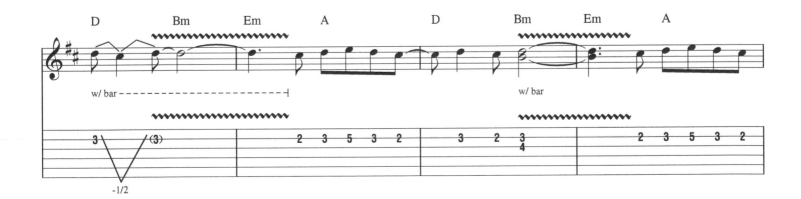

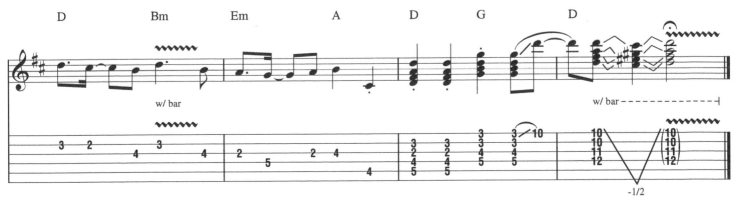

Pipeline

By Bob Spickard and Brian Carman

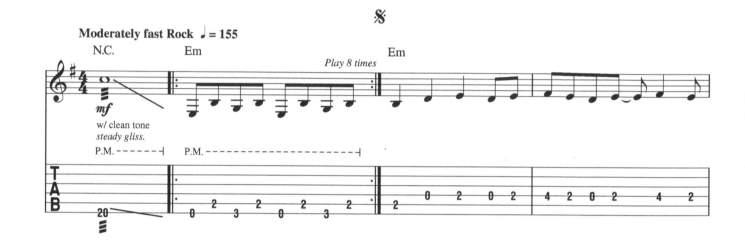

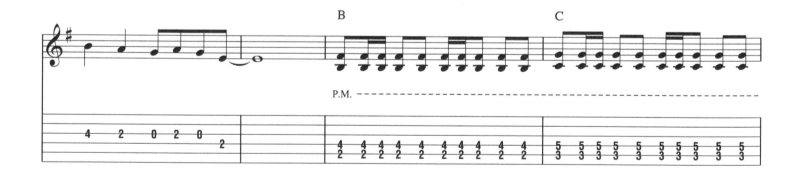

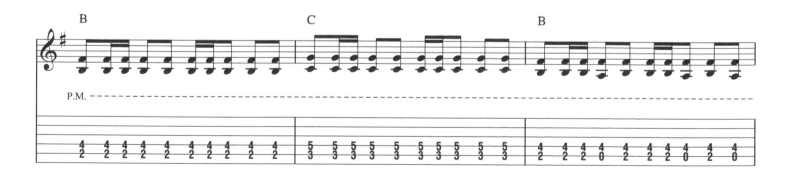

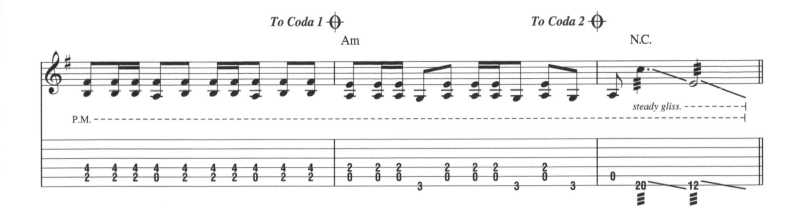

6th time, D.S. al Coda 1

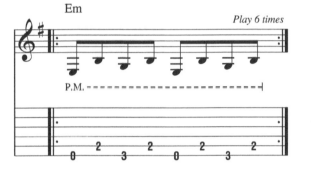

⊕ **Coda 1**

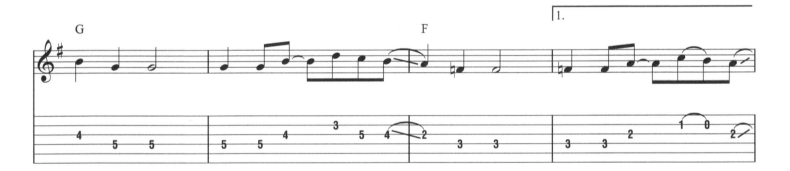

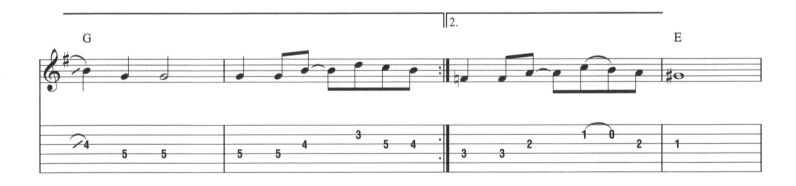

6th time, D.S. al Coda 2

⊕ **Coda 2**

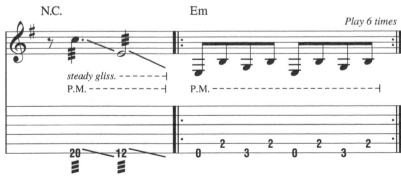

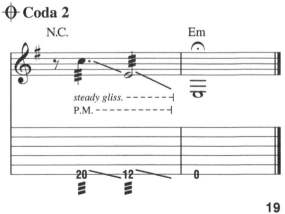

Secret Agent Man

Words and Music by P.F. Sloan and Steve Barri

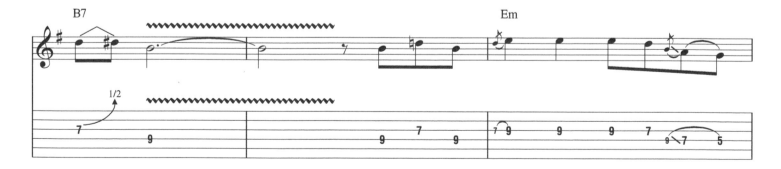

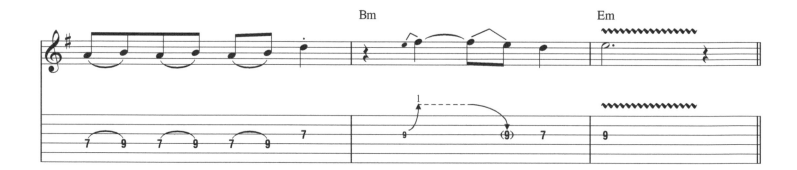

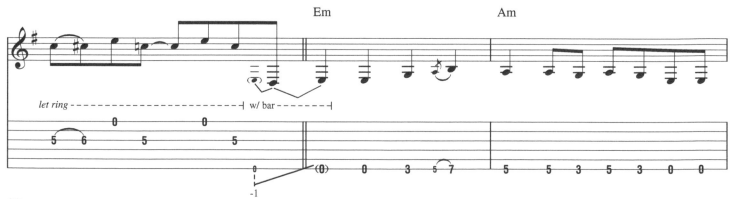

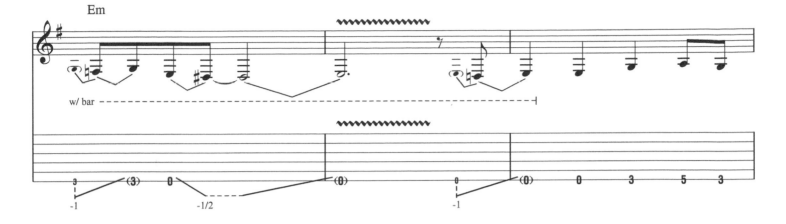

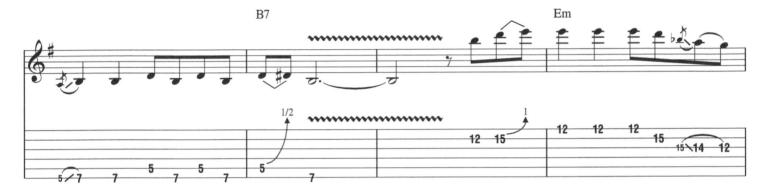

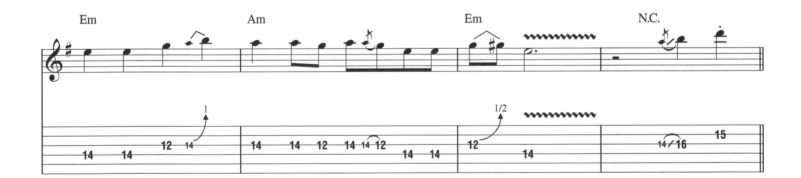

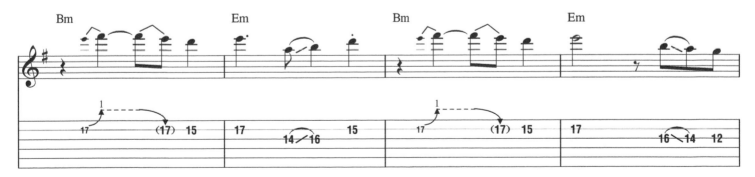

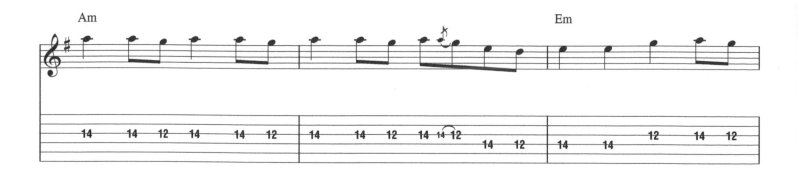

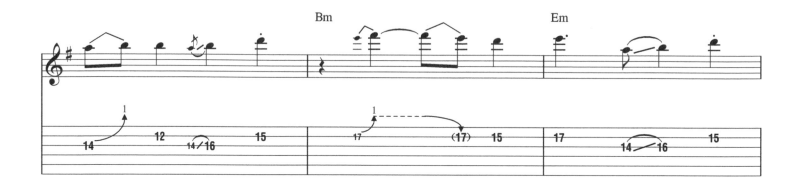

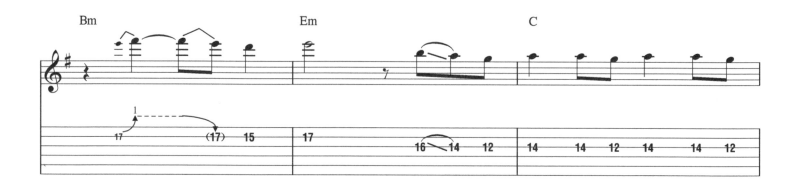

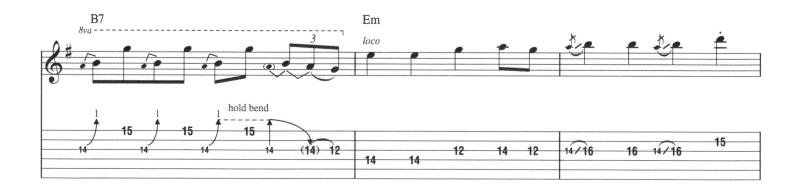

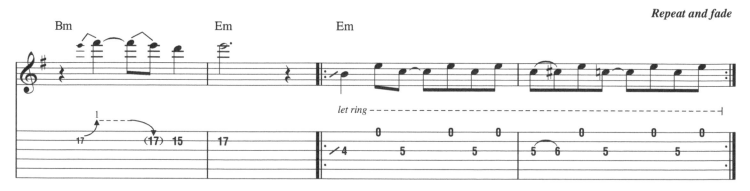

Walk Don't Run

By Johnny Smith

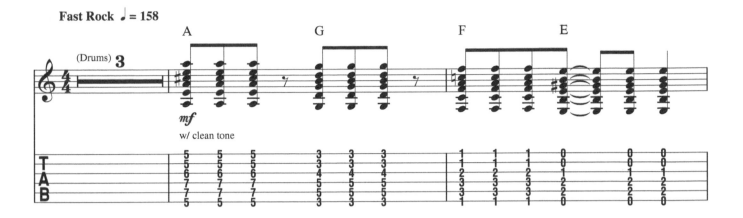

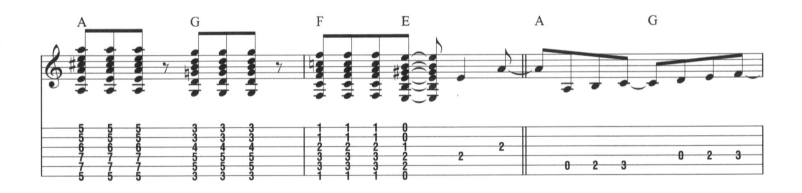

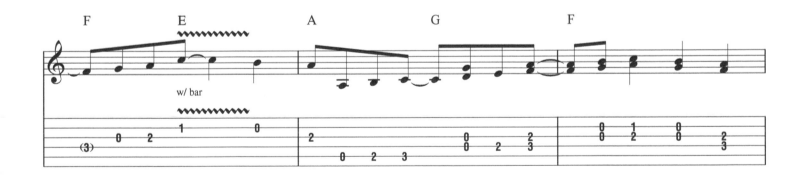

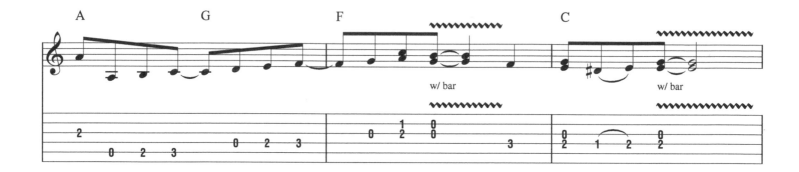

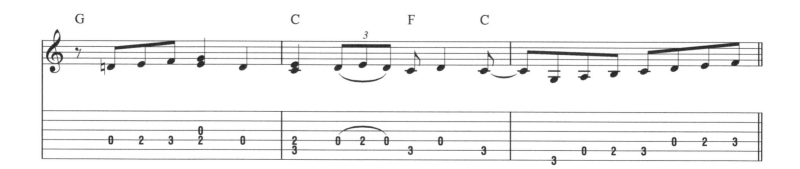

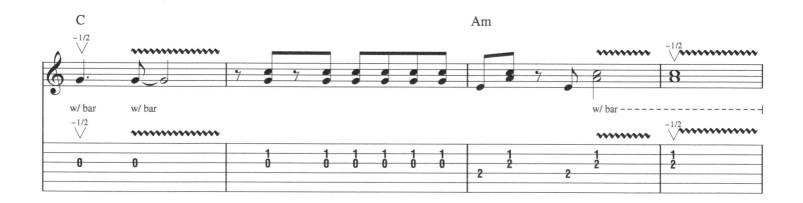

To Coda ⊕

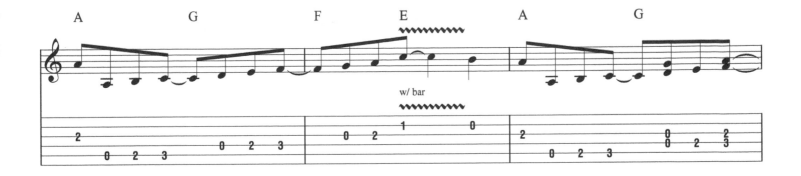

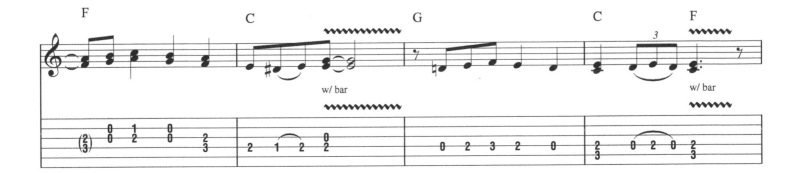

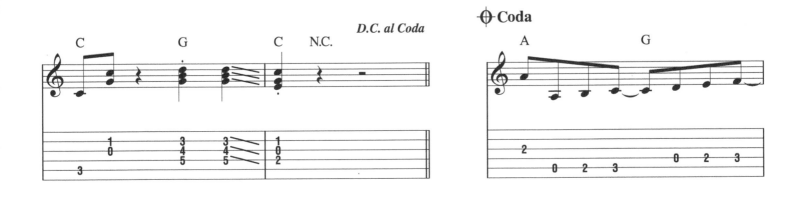

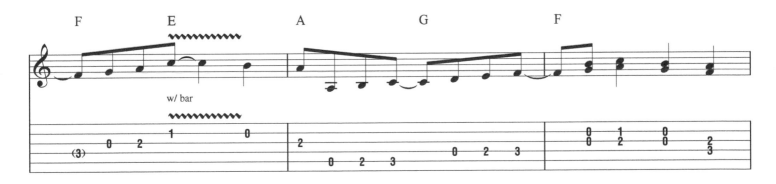

Wipe Out

By The Surfaris

Moderately fast ♩ = 162

(Tom-tom)

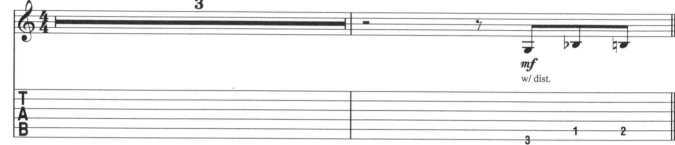

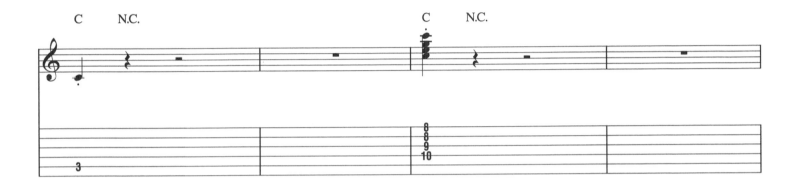

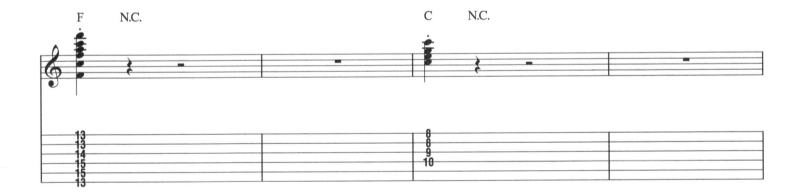

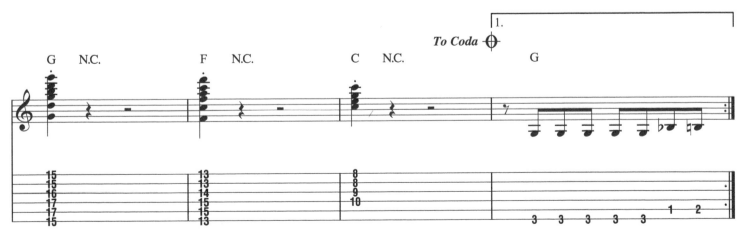

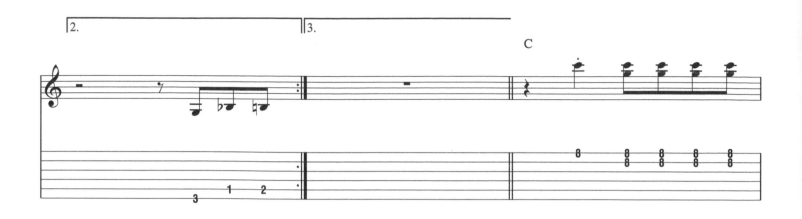

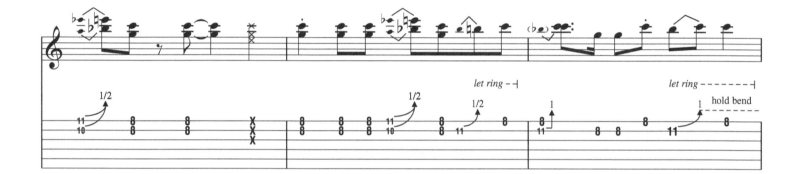

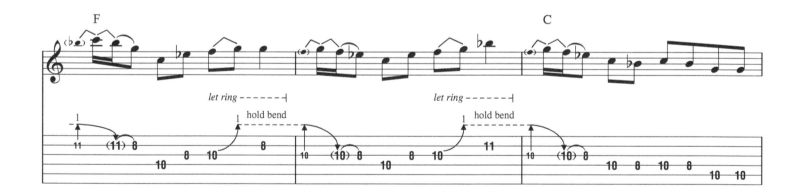

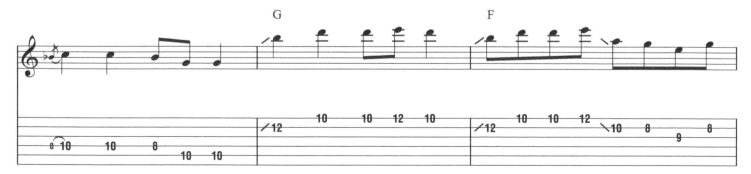

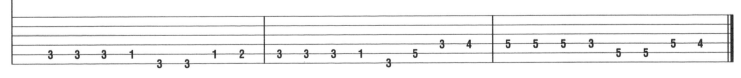

Guitar Notation Legend

15 />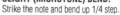

THE MUSICAL STAFF shows pitches and rhythms and is divided by bar lines into measures. Pitches are named after the first seven letters of the alphabet.

TABLATURE graphically represents the guitar fingerboard. Each horizontal line represents a string, and each number represents a fret.

4th string, 2nd fret   1st & 2nd strings open, played together   open D chord

---

HALF-STEP BEND: Strike the note and bend up 1/2 step.

WHOLE-STEP BEND: Strike the note and bend up one step.

GRACE NOTE BEND: Strike the note and bend up as indicated. The first note does not take up any time.

SLIGHT (MICROTONE) BEND: Strike the note and bend up 1/4 step.

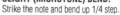

BEND AND RELEASE: Strike the note and bend up as indicated, then release back to the original note. Only the first note is struck.

PRE-BEND: Bend the note as indicated, then strike it.

VIBRATO: The string is vibrated by rapidly bending and releasing the note with the fretting hand.

PALM MUTING: The note is partially muted by the pick hand lightly touching the string(s) just before the bridge.

HAMMER-ON: Strike the first (lower) note with one finger, then sound the higher note (on the same string) with another finger by fretting it without picking.

PULL-OFF: Place both fingers on the notes to be sounded. Strike the first note and without picking, pull the finger off to sound the second (lower) note.

LEGATO SLIDE: Strike the first note and then slide the same fret-hand finger up or down to the second note. The second note is not struck.

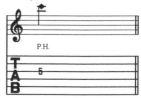

SHIFT SLIDE: Same as legato slide, except the second note is struck.

TRILL: Very rapidly alternate between the notes indicated by continuously hammering on and pulling off.

TAPPING: Hammer ("tap") the fret indicated with the pick-hand index or middle finger and pull off to the note fretted by the fret hand.

NATURAL HARMONIC: Strike the note while the fret-hand lightly touches the string directly over the fret indicated.

PINCH HARMONIC: The note is fretted normally and a harmonic is produced by adding the edge of the thumb or the tip of the index finger of the pick hand to the normal pick attack.

TREMOLO PICKING: The note is picked as rapidly and continuously as possible.

VIBRATO BAR DIVE AND RETURN:
The pitch of the note or chord is dropped a specified number of steps (in rhythm) then returned to the original pitch.

VIBRATO BAR SCOOP: Depress the bar just before striking the note, then quickly release the bar.

VIBRATO BAR DIP: Strike the note and then immediately drop a specified number of steps, then release back to the original pitch.

Additional Musical Definitions

 (accent) • Accentuate note (play it louder)

Fill   • Label used to identify a brief melodic figure which is to be inserted into the arrangement.

 (staccato) • Play the note short

N.C.   • No Chord

D.S. al Coda • Go back to the sign (𝄋), then play until the measure marked *"To Coda,"* then skip to the section labelled *"Coda."*

 • Repeat measures between signs.

D.C. al Fine • Go back to the beginning of the song and play until the measure marked *"Fine"* (end).

 • When a repeated section has different endings, play the first ending only the first time and the second ending only the second time.

14 />

10 />